ELEPHANT

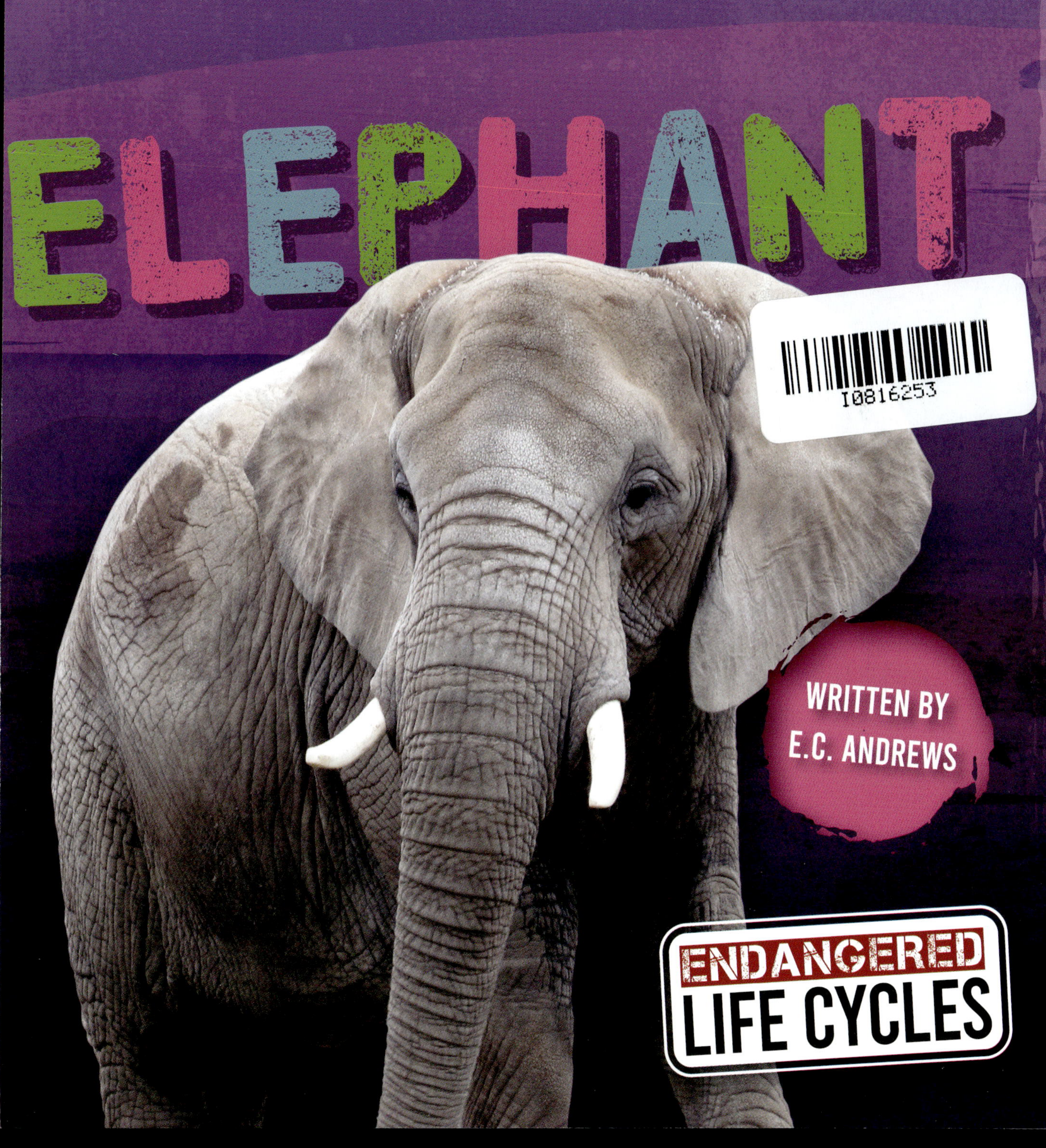

Library of Congress Control Number:
The Library of Congress Control Number is available on the Library of Congress website.

ISBN
979-8-89359-311-2 (library bound)
979-8-89359-395-2 (paperback)
979-8-89359-370-9 (epub)
979-8-89359-341-9 (hosted ebook)

Printed in the United States of America
Mankato, MN
092025

sales@northstareditions.com
888-417-0195

Written by:
E.C. Andrews

Edited by:
Rebecca Phillips-Bartlett

Designed by:
Ker Ker Lee

Photo Credits – Images are courtesy of Shutterstock.com. With thanks to Getty Images, Thinkstock Photo and iStockphoto.

Cover – Elina Litovkinam, Maciej Czekajewski, Richard Peterson, VVadi4ka, MIKHAIL GRACHIKOV. Recurring – bum katya, imaginasty, VVadi4ka, Elina Litovkina, Maciej Czekajewski. 4–5 – PCH.Vector. 6–7 – hansen.matthew.d, Piotr Poznan, Roger de la Harpe, Nilanka Sampath. 8–9 – Gunter Nuyts, OliverZeid. 10–11 – Sahan Avishka, Hyserb, Greenort. 12–13 – Jan Tobolka, Efimova Anna. 14–15 – John Michael Vosloo, powell'sPoint. 16–17 – Zhukova Valentyna, Marcin Osman. 18–19 – Johan W. Elzenga, michaldp90. 20–21 – MD_Photography, Villiers Steyn. 22–23 – Akarawut, Maples Images.

CONTENTS

WORDS THAT LOOK LIKE THIS CAN BE FOUND IN THE GLOSSARY ON PAGE 24.

WHAT IS A LIFE CYCLE?

Animals, plants, and people are living things. Living things change and grow. They go through different stages. These stages make up a life cycle.

Animals are small when they are born. They grow bigger as their lives go on. Most adult animals have offspring. This process allows the life cycle to continue.

ELEPHANTS

Elephants are large mammals. They live in Africa and Asia. They live in groups called herds. Each herd has a female in charge. There are three species of elephant.

The three elephant species are the African savanna elephant, the African forest elephant, and the Asian elephant. African savanna elephants are the largest land mammals in the world.

ENDANGERED ANIMALS

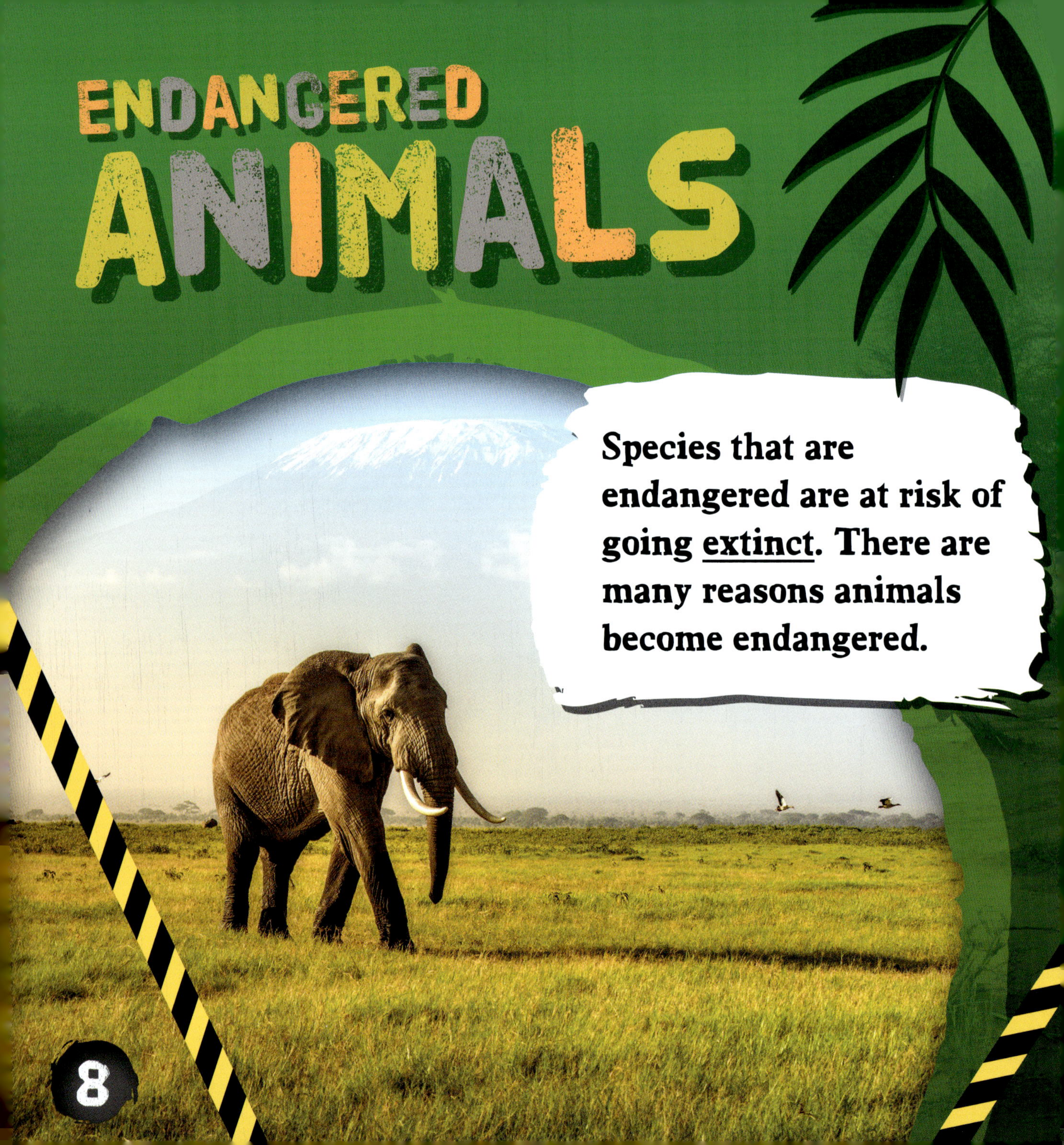

Species that are endangered are at risk of going extinct. There are many reasons animals become endangered.

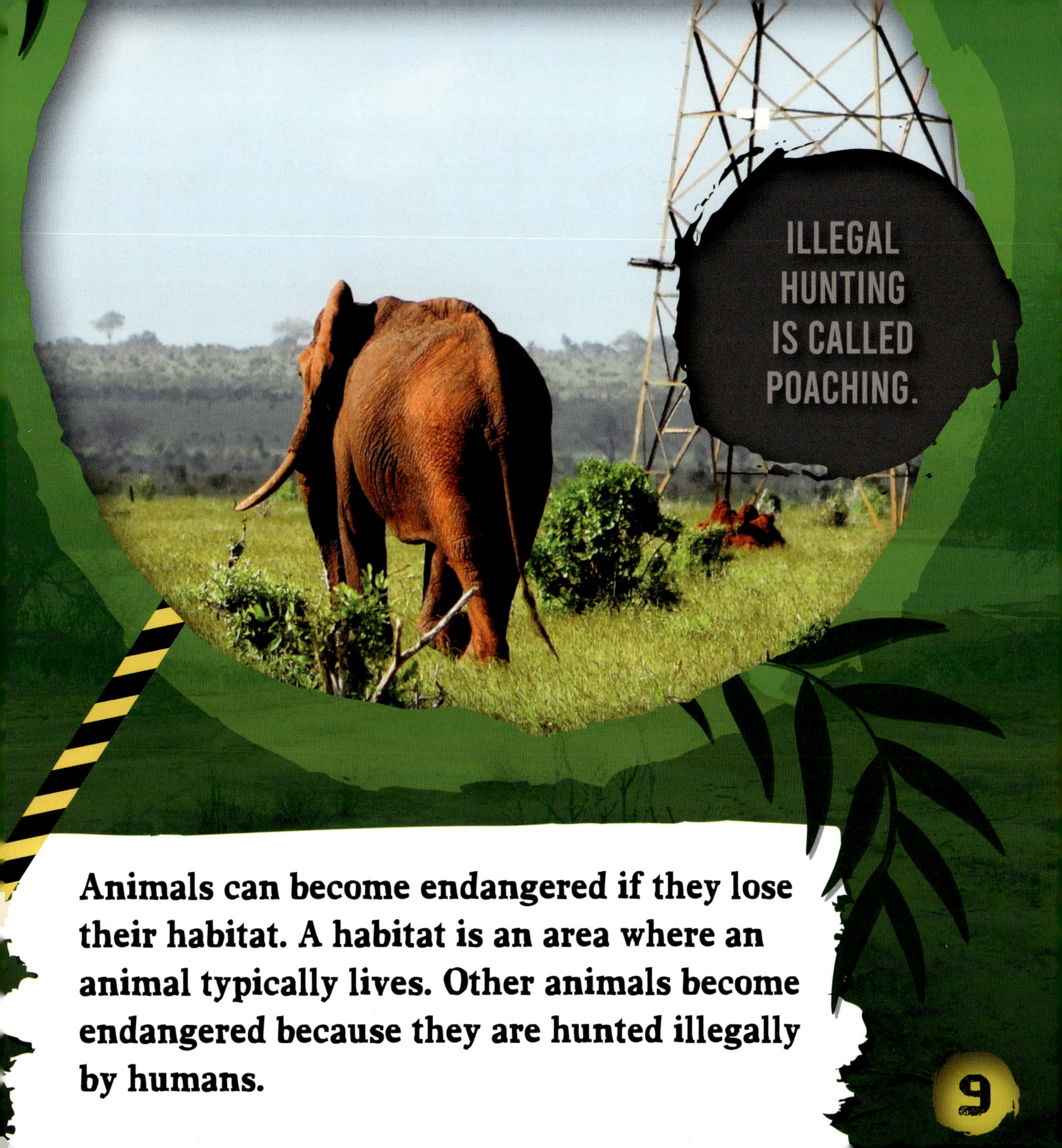

Animals can become endangered if they lose their habitat. A habitat is an area where an animal typically lives. Other animals become endangered because they are hunted illegally by humans.

THE LIFE CYCLE BEGINS

To help elephants, it is important to understand their life cycles. Adult elephants find mates. Then most have offspring. This keeps the life cycle going.

A BABY ELEPHANT IS CALLED A CALF.

Elephants may start having calves when they are 10 to 20 years old. They have calves every four to five years. They usually have only one calf at a time.

BEING BORN

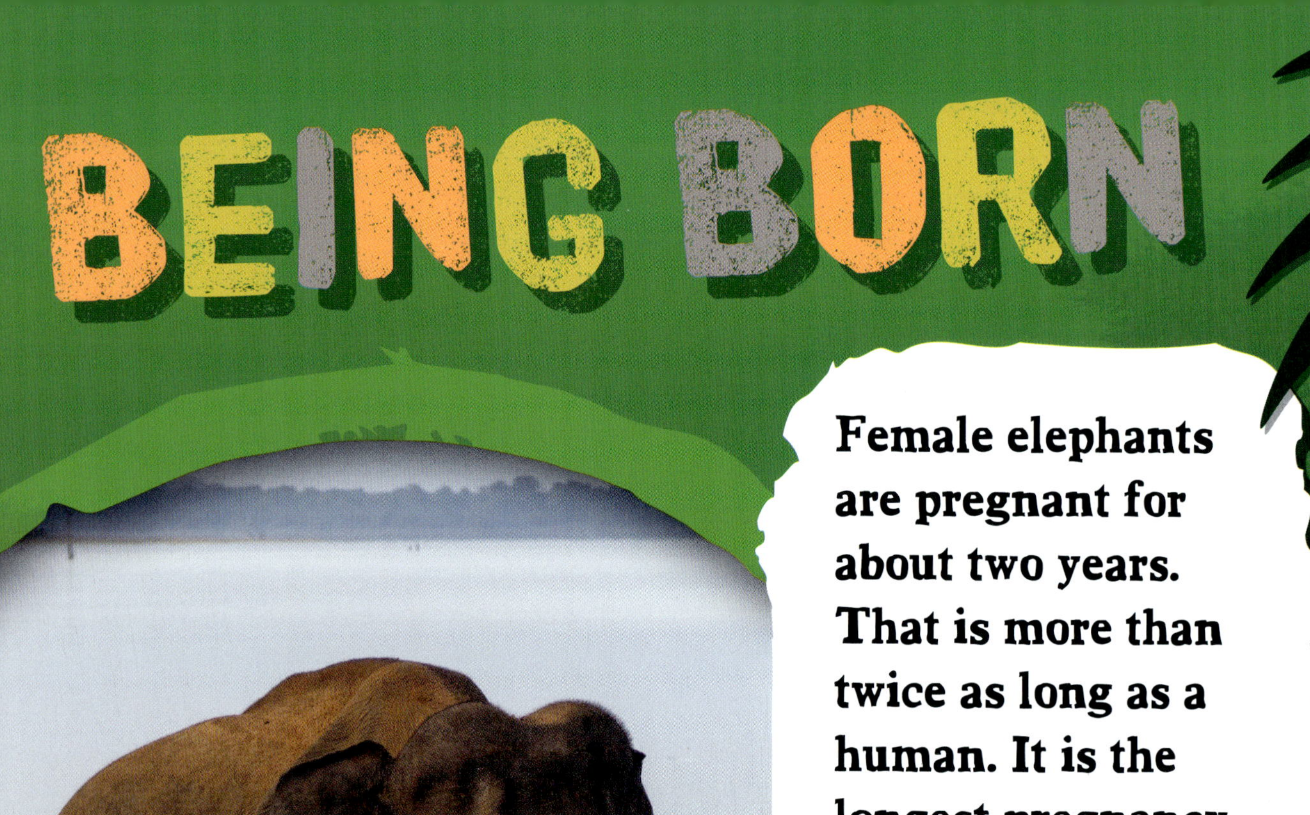

Female elephants are pregnant for about two years. That is more than twice as long as a human. It is the longest pregnancy of any mammal.

THIS ELEPHANT IS PREGNANT.

Elephants surround the mother while she is giving birth. They protect her. It can take days for an elephant to give birth.

NEWBORN CALVES

A newborn calf relies on its mother for protection. The females in the herd work together to raise the calf.

Calves can stand up 20 minutes after they are born. They can walk within a few hours. Calves are born with lots of hair. This hair helps protect them from the sun.

CALVES LOSE MOST OF THEIR HAIR AS THEY GROW UP.

GROWING UP

Elephants have strong bonds with their herds. Young calves stay close to their mothers. Mothers comfort their calves when they are upset.

Calves drink their mother's milk for the first few years of their lives. Then they start eating plants. The herd teaches calves how to find food.

ADULT LIFE

Most elephants have tusks. They use their tusks to dig and find food. Elephants also use their tusks to lift things and fight off danger.

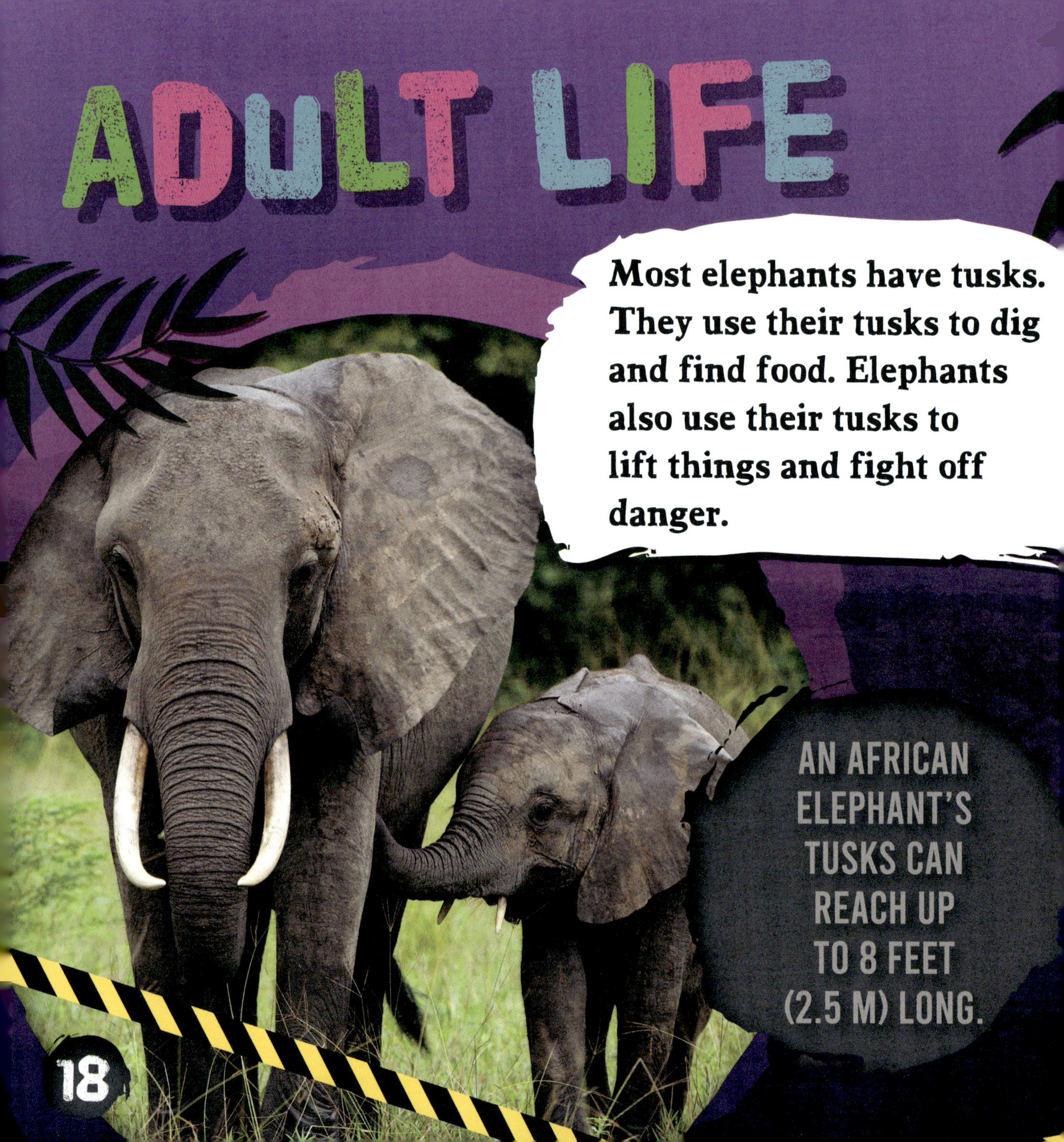

AN AFRICAN ELEPHANT'S TUSKS CAN REACH UP TO 8 FEET (2.5 M) LONG.

Adult males leave their herd to find mates. Female elephants stay in the herd they were born in.

IN THE WILD, SOME ELEPHANTS LIVE FOR UP TO 70 YEARS.

DANGERS

Many elephants are losing their habitats to deforestation. Deforestation is when humans remove forests so they can use the land to grow food and build things.

ELEPHANT TUSKS ARE MADE OF IVORY.

Poaching is another danger to elephants. Poachers hunt elephants for their tusks. They sell the tusks for money. Elephants have young very slowly. This makes it difficult for elephants to continue their life cycle.

THE LIFE CYCLE CONTINUES

Many people are working hard to protect elephants. Some help regrow forests. Others catch poachers and remove animal traps.

A CONSERVATIONIST IS SOMEONE WHO PROTECTS ANIMALS AND THE ENVIRONMENT.

There are some small things you can do to help elephants.

- Do not buy products made of ivory.
- Avoid products that are made because of deforestation, such as palm oil.

TOGETHER, WE CAN HELP THE ELEPHANT'S LIFE CYCLE CONTINUE!

GLOSSARY

BONDS relationships based on love, friendship, and loyalty

ENVIRONMENT the natural world

EXTINCT none left in the world

MAMMALS animals that are warm-blooded, have a backbone, and produce milk to feed their children

MATES partners of the same species that animals produce young with

OFFSPRING the young of an animal, a person, or a plant

SPECIES a group of very similar animals or plants that can create young together

INDEX